SUMMER
IN JANE'S GARDEN

Written by

JANE HUML

Illustrated by

LOIS HUML DURDA

ISBN 978-1-63525-372-6 (Paperback)
ISBN 978-1-63525-373-3 (Digital)

Christian Faith Publishing, Inc.
296 Chestnut Street
Meadville, PA 16335
www.christianfaithpublishing.com

Printed in the United States of America

Dedicated to our grandchildren

Jonathan
Olivia
Dana
Darrin
Jessica
Leah
Cheyenne
Anna
Andie
Vivienne

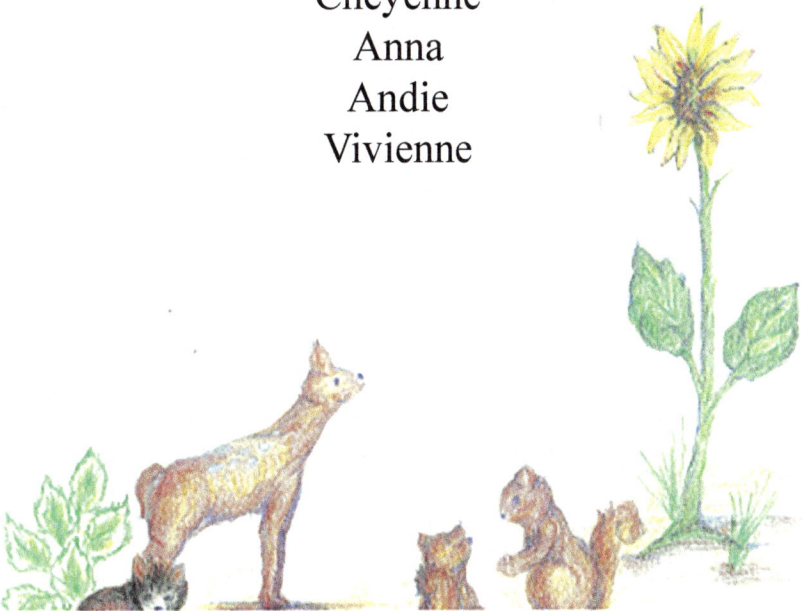

Lisi Anthus

Lisianthus is a perennial flower that blooms in a variety of colors: white, pink, purple. It is native to the southern American prairies.

Lisi Anthus came to live in Jane's garden.

She happily attended to the
ferns and spring flowers.

Lisi watches the flowers. She eyes feathery astilbes—
pink, white, and red.

She smiles over bright orange Oriental lilies, round
pink phlox, tall gladiolas, and white daisies with
yellow centers.

Close to the ground, she spies chipmunks and mice nibbling red strawberries.

Above them, wild purple thistle reaches for the sky.

Oh no! Here comes a family of deer to feast on the hosta!

Perhaps Jane won't mind if they do not eat the squash.

All creatures must eat after all: mice, deer, chipmunks, squirrels, raccoons, and possums.

Lisi watches the vegetables grow. The plants grow taller and blossom. Honeybees and bumblebees come to sip nectar and collect pollen, returning to their hives to manufacture the honey.

Every day, the garden plants change. Flowers wither and vegetables begin to grow.

Rains come in June bringing
warm water to quench the thirst
of the growing plants.

Robins fly down to feast on
worms at Lisi's feet.

At last!

The sun comes out again!

Goldfinches arrive to taste the yellow sunflower petals.

Lisi's eyes light up when she hears the happy songs of wrens, sparrows, and chickadees as they pick the best seeds for their dinners.

She laughs at Mr. Blue Jay splashing in the birdbath…

…and looks tenderly as Mr. and Mrs. Cardinal teach their babies to fly…

…and admires the speedy humming birds flitting from pink petunias as to red geranium, sipping nectar for breakfast.

The days are hot and long in July.

Nights are not much cooler.

Lisi waves to Blue Heron, the weather vane as he bobs his head amid the scarlet chrysanthemums. And then…

...to the butterflies visiting the purple and pink coneflowers as they celebrate midsummer before laying their eggs on the leaves and flying south.

Look who else is watching Jane's garden grow! It's that deer family! Count them! 1, 2, 3, 4, 5.

They are nibbling the leaves of Jane's tomatoes and squash.

The garden grows. Jane thinks the animals are taking more than their share! Jane is not happy.

Rabbits prefer nibbling the green beans. Mamma shows her bunnies how to pick the best ones.

Jane sprays hot pepper on the leaves to discourage those pesky visitors. Rabbits visit the neighbor's garden until the spray is washed away by the next rain.

Note:

Hot pepper spray does not hurt the animals; they just don't like the taste.

Across the path is the herb garden: chives, oregano, basil, and parsley.

Jane will use the herbs for cooking.

Today bees and butterflies gather the pollen.

Lisi looks over to the neighbor's yard and sees a new friend watching over that garden.
It's Clyde!

Jane harvests, sharing with the greedy groundhog, the rabbit family, and her neighbors.

Autumn will come with cooler weather. Flowers return to their roots until next year when a new garden will be planted.

The End.

Wait till next spring.

ABOUT THE AUTHOR

Jane is a retired special education teacher from Cleveland, Ohio. She was born and raised in Cleveland and attended Cleveland public schools where she later taught. She lived in Shoreline, Connecticut for about a dozen years where she learned to work with special needs adults at a company called VISTA (Vocational Life Skills Center) and walked the beach every day. She has a sister who is a professional artist and therefore, did the illustrations for *Summer in Jane's Garden*, and a brother who is a retired electrician. She also has three grown sons, six grandchildren, and one great granddaughter.

Today, I still live a short walk from water. This time, it's Lake Erie again.

CPSIA information can be obtained
at www.ICGtesting.com
Printed in the USA
BVOW10s1833201216

471393BV00015B/257/P

9 781635 253726